Resolving Childhood Trauma

A Parent's Guide to Helping Traumatized Children Develop Resilience: Integrating the Mind, Body, and Spirit for Recovery and Development

Michele L. Valdez

Introducing the exclusive and captivating world of Michele L. Valdez. Immerse yourself in the timeless elegance and creativity that defines our brand. Experience the unparalleled craftsmanship and attention to detail that sets us apart. Discover the essence of sophistication and style with our exquisite collection. Copyright © 2024 Michele L. Valdez

Experience the exclusivity of our copyrighted content. Introducing an extraordinary publication that captivates the mind and sparks inspiration. This masterpiece is protected by the highest standards of copyright law. Reproduction, distribution, or transmission in any form or by any means is strictly prohibited without the prior written permission of the esteemed publisher. However, in the realm of critical reviews and select non-commercial uses, brief quotations may be embraced. Unlock the power of knowledge while respecting the rights of the visionary creators.

Table of Contents

RESOLVING CHILDHOOD TRAUMA 1

PREFACE 4

INTRODUCTION 11

CHAPTER 1 14
    UNLOCK THE SECRETS TO SUCCESSFUL PARENTING FOR CHILDREN WITH TRAUMA 14
    DISCOVER THE TELLTALE SYMPTOMS OF TRAUMA IN CHILDREN 18

CHAPTER 2 24
    THE IMPACT OF TRAUMA IN CHILDHOOD 24
    CAUSES AND EFFECTS OF TRAUMA ON THE GROWTH AND CONDUCT OF CHILDREN. 32

CHAPTER 3 40
    HOW TO PROVIDE COMPREHENSIVE REHAB FOR CHILDREN. 40

CHAPTER 4 64
    DISCOVER THE ESSENTIAL GUIDE TO CARING FOR TRAUMATIZED CHILDREN. 64
    FOUR WAYS TO BEGIN HEALING FROM TRAUMA DURING CHILDHOOD. 77

CHAPTER 5 83
    CARING FOR CHILDREN WHO HAVE EXPERIENCED TRAUMA 83
    WAYS TO SUPPORT A TRAUMATIZED CHILD IN AN EDUCATIONAL SETTING. 86

ACKNOWLEDGEMENTS 96

Preface

Are you a dedicated parent or caregiver bravely navigating the complex and transformative journey of raising a child who has encountered the hardships of trauma? Are you in search of expert guidance and unwavering support to help you understand and meet your child's unique needs while fostering their resilience? Introducing our revolutionary masterpiece, "Resolving Childhood Trauma: A Parent's Guide to Helping Traumatized Children Develop Resilience: Integrating the Mind, Body, and Spirit for Recovery and Development." Prepare to embark on an extraordinary odyssey of transformation, as we unveil the ultimate roadmap to healing and personal growth.

Discover the incredible challenges that children encounter in our modern world, as they navigate through adversities that leave an indelible mark on their lives. Discover the profound impact that abuse, neglect, and other traumatic events can have on one's emotional, psychological, and social well-being. Uncover the lasting imprints that these experiences can leave behind. Are you a parent feeling overwhelmed and unsure of how to best support your children through life's challenges? Look no further! We understand the struggles you face and are here to help. Introducing "Unlock the Power Within" - your ultimate guiding light amidst the shadows of uncertainty.

Unleash the Power of Resilient Parenting with Empowering Strategies

Discover the invaluable strategies for resilient parenting that lie at the heart of "Resolving Childhood Trauma". Uncover a treasure trove of empowering techniques that will transform your parenting journey. Unlock the extraordinary potential within your child's life with the unwavering belief that every parent possesses the remarkable ability to overcome any obstacle and create a profoundly positive impact. Introducing our groundbreaking book that combines cutting-edge research in neuroscience, psychology, and trauma-informed care. Packed with invaluable tools and actionable advice, it equips you with the knowledge and skills to confidently navigate the intricate world of trauma, all while embracing a compassionate approach.

Experience the Power of Holistic Healing

Introducing "Resolving Childhood Trauma" - the groundbreaking parenting guide that revolutionizes the way we heal. Unlike any other guide out there, it takes a holistic approach, ensuring that every aspect of your child's well-being is nurtured and restored. Discover the profound impact of trauma on not only the individual, but also the intricate web of relationships within the family system. Discover the transformative power of our book, which goes beyond just supporting your child. It provides invaluable guidance for fostering healing and growth within yourself and your family. Unlock the secrets to creating a harmonious and thriving family dynamic with our expertly crafted pages. Discover the power of our heartfelt narratives, expert insights, and innovative practices as we guide you on a transformative journey. Learn how to turn trauma into triumph and emerge as a stronger, more resilient version of yourself. Join us and unlock your true potential.

Embark on an Unforgettable Journey of Transformation

Experience a life-changing odyssey of self-discovery as you immerse yourself in the captivating world of "Resolving Childhood Trauma." Prepare to embark on a transformative journey as you delve into each meticulously crafted chapter, meticulously designed to empower you with invaluable insights and equip you with the tools to unlock your inner strength and resilience. Through a series of thought-provoking exercises, you will be inspired to tap into your untapped potential and embrace the challenges that lie ahead. Embark on a transformative journey towards healing and growth as you delve into the profound effects of trauma on the developing brain. Uncover a treasure trove of knowledge and inspiration that will ignite your passion for fostering healthy attachment and resilience. Prepare to be empowered as you navigate the path towards a brighter future.

Experience the power of real-life stories that inspire hope and bring about healing. Discover the incredible journeys of individuals who have overcome adversity and found strength in the face of challenges. Immerse yourself in these compelling narratives that will touch your heart and leave you feeling uplifted. Explore the transformative power of hope and healing through these captivating

Embark on a transformative journey with "Resolving Childhood Trauma," where you'll be captivated by the inspiring tales of triumph and restoration shared by experienced parents and caregivers who have traversed the very same path as you. Brace yourself for a powerful exploration of hope and healing that will leave you feeling inspired and empowered. Immerse yourself in these captivating stories that shine like beacons, illuminating the darkest corners. They provide inspiring glimpses into the realm of endless possibilities, reminding us of the extraordinary strength of resilience and the transformative power of love. Discover the inspiring tales of triumph over adversity and the profound bonds formed with our children. These captivating stories serve as a powerful reminder that we are never alone in our quest for healing.

Experience the Power of the Movement

Introducing "Resolving Childhood Trauma" - not just a book, but a powerful movement towards healing and transformation. Experience the power of unity and support by joining our exclusive community of resilient parents and caregivers. Together, we will embark on an extraordinary journey filled with strength, compassion, and shared experiences. Discover a world of connection and support through our online forums, vibrant support groups, and exciting live events. Connect with like-minded individuals who understand your experiences and share your aspirations. Join our community today and unlock the power of connection. Join us on a transformative journey as we harness the power of words to ignite a wave of healing and hope that will reverberate far beyond the confines of our book. Together, we will create a ripple effect that touches lives and inspires change.

Embark on Your Journey Today

Get ready to unleash the untapped potential within you

and turn your past struggles into incredible victories. Prepare to embark on a journey of personal growth and empowerment like never before. Embark on a transformative path towards healing and personal growth with the remarkable book "Resolving Childhood Trauma". Don't wait any longer to take the first crucial step - order your copy today and unlock a brighter future. Prepare to embark on a transformative journey as you delve into the pages of this remarkable book. Each turn of the page will unveil a treasure trove of profound insights, boundless inspiration, and invaluable strategies that will empower you to gracefully navigate the intricate labyrinth of trauma. With unwavering resilience, you will conquer every challenge that comes your way. Brace yourself for a life-changing experience! Unlock the extraordinary potential that lies within your grasp and seize the opportunity to revolutionize not only your own life, but also the lives of your precious children. Don't delay any longer – take action now and witness the incredible transformation that awaits you. Experience the power of unlocking it today.

Introduction

Introducing "Resolving Childhood Trauma" by the esteemed psychologist Michele L. Valdez - a revolutionary guide that paves the way to healing deep-seated wounds from the past and rediscovering a future brimming with hope and unwavering strength. Experience the groundbreaking expertise of Dr. Richards as he unveils a revolutionary approach to conquering childhood trauma. With a wealth of clinical experience and cutting-edge advancements in trauma therapy, Dr. Richards empowers survivors to liberate themselves from the shackles of their past and embrace a future filled with boundless joy and fulfillment.

Prepare to be captivated by Michele L. Valdez's extraordinary guide, as she fearlessly delves into the complex depths of childhood trauma. With unwavering compassion, Valdez unveils the profound effects it has on our mental, emotional, and physical well-being. Prepare to be captivated by a collection of heartfelt real-life stories and enlightened by cutting-edge scientific insights.

Brace yourself for a transformative journey of self-discovery and empowerment, expertly guided by her wise and compassionate words.

Discover the profound journey of healing as "Resolving Childhood Trauma" delves into the depths of trauma, unearthing its origins and paving the way for resilience. With a treasure trove of practical strategies and evidence-based techniques, this remarkable guide will navigate you through the intricate complexities of healing. Discover the transformative power of cultivating self-compassion, rebuilding shattered trust, and forging authentic connections with others. Unlock the secrets to personal growth and fulfillment as you embark on a journey of self-discovery and healing. Experience the transformative power of Michele L. Valdez's compassionate and clear guidance as she equips readers with the essential tools to rewrite their stories and reclaim their true power. Discover a path to personal growth and empowerment like never before.

Introducing the ultimate guide to healing and wholeness! No matter if you've experienced childhood trauma, are a caring caregiver, or a mental health professional seeking innovative approaches, this book is your must-have companion. Discover the transformative power within its pages and embark on a journey towards complete well-being.

Uncover the hidden secrets that hold the power to unlock profound healing and transformative change in the groundbreaking masterpiece, "Resolving Childhood Trauma." Experience the transformative power of embracing your journey from mere survival to flourishing, as you unlock a future brimming with endless possibilities and profound purpose.

Chapter 1

Unlock the Secrets to Successful Parenting for Children with Trauma

Experience the transformative power of creating a safe and loving environment for children who have faced traumatic events. Discover the essential nurturing environment every parent must provide for their children. Discover the transformative power of understanding trauma's impact on children. Without this knowledge, parents may unintentionally misinterpret their child's behavior, leading to frustration and resentment. Equip yourself with the insights you need to foster a deeper connection with your child.

Discover the innovative approach to managing challenging behavior that guarantees results. Say goodbye to ineffective methods and potential harm. Experience the difference today! Introducing our comprehensive factsheet that delves into the intricate world of trauma, shedding light on its profound impact on the tender hearts and minds of children and youngsters.

Discover invaluable insights and expert advice on how to empower your beloved kids on their journey towards healing and resilience.

Supercharge your understanding of stress and unlock the key to supporting your child's recovery. Discover how this newfound knowledge can strengthen your relationship with your little one and bring harmony to your entire family unit.

Discover the profound concept of Trauma.

Experience the profound impact of trauma, an intense emotional reaction triggered by a harrowing event that poses a grave threat or inflicts harm. Experience the profound impact that can be inflicted upon a child or their loved ones, whether it be through physical or psychological harm. This damage, whether tangible or acknowledged, has the power to pose a threat that should not be taken lightly.

Experience the profound impact of trauma, a result of personal events or connections to a series of experiences over time.

Introducing a world of potentially traumatic events that can leave a lasting impact on individuals. Brace yourself for a range of experiences that include abuse in all its forms - physical, romantic, and psychological. Prepare to delve into the depths of neglect, where the absence of care can leave scars that never truly heal. And let us not forget the far-reaching consequences of poverty, where the harsh realities of homelessness and low sustainability cast a shadow over lives. Explore the complexities of these events and the profound effects they can have on the human spirit.

Introducing the Challenges of Life:

- Experience the heart-wrenching separation from your loved ones.

- Confront the harsh reality of bullying and its detrimental effects.

- Bear witness to the distressing problems faced by those you hold dear, such as domestic or community assault.

- Introducing the unpredictable forces of nature and unforeseen accidents that can disrupt our lives. Additionally, the delicate balance of stable parenting can be affected by dependencies or mental illness.

Discover how the child welfare system can inadvertently compound trauma for vulnerable children. Experience the undeniable truth of a child's first separation from home and family, just as powerful as any additional placements.

Unleash the Power of Addressing Untreated Trauma

Discover the incredible resilience of children. Experience the exhilarating rush of growth and development as stress weaves its way into their lives. From bidding farewell to caregivers embarking on a well-deserved vacation, to the triumphant moment of buttoning a shirt for the very first time, and the nerve-wracking anticipation before a game or performance, these moments of anxiety fuel their young minds to blossom and acquire new skills.

Discover the undeniable truth: trauma strikes when a child's natural resilience is overpowered by the weight of a distressing encounter, whether it be abuse, neglect, or relentless bullying. Experience the incredible power of these events as they ignite a primal "fight, air travel, or freeze" response within your body. Witness the remarkable adjustments that take place, including a surge in heart rate and a rise in bloodstream pressure. Prepare to be amazed by the profound changes in the way your mind perceives and responds to the world.

Discover the remarkable resilience of a child's body and brain as they swiftly bounce back from potentially traumatic experiences, leaving no lasting damage behind. Discover how injury can hinder normal development and have lasting effects on children.

Discover the Telltale Symptoms of Trauma in Children

During the challenging week following a distressing event or tragic loss in the lives of children, we recognize the immense efforts of parents and teachers in supporting kids to navigate their grief and anxiety in a positive and constructive manner. Introducing our expert tips on engaging children in a calm and nurturing conversation about their emotions. While it may seem challenging, the impact it can have on children is truly remarkable.

Discover the unfortunate reality: certain children are at even greater risk of enduring lasting consequences from a distressing incident. This includes those who have experienced the heart-wrenching loss of friends or classmates, and have had to grapple with the profound emotions and grief that accompany such a loss.

"Discover the profound impact that a child's experience at a gathering can have, and how those around them handle it can potentially be traumatizing," reveals Dr. Jerry Bubrick, a renowned psychologist at the Child Brain Institute. Discover the power of unexpected information! When households stumble upon it unintentionally, parents may find themselves caught off guard, leading to highly emotional reactions that can have a lasting impact on their children. Experience the full power of television coverage and be captivated by the surprising newspaper headlines that will magnify the impact of any troubling event or reduction.

As you strive to provide solace and reassurance to children, it is of utmost importance to recognize the indications of detrimental coping mechanisms that may indicate the necessity of consulting a professional. Discover the startling truth: even in the most extreme circumstances, children are not immune to the devastating effects of post-traumatic stress disorder. But it doesn't stop there. Even milder symptoms resembling PTSD can cast a dark shadow over a child's life, robbing them of the happiness and joy they deserve. Discover the essential signs to consider and unlock the key things to remember.

Introducing: Normal Grief

"Discover the unique journey of grief," advises Dr. Bubrick, emphasizing that the speed at which one grieves varies for each individual. Whether it's an immediate response or a seemingly inadequate one, it does not determine the resilience of a child in dealing with loss. "Discover the hidden dangers of apparent coping in youngsters," warns our expert. According to him, even if they seem fine now, they may still experience an unhealthy response in the future.

Discover the unique rhythm of grief that resonates within each individual.

Discover the possibility that you could be the indicator of their exceptional handling. Discover the power of making a lasting impact on our children's lives by taking action immediately after the event. Often, the true effects of your actions may not become apparent until three to six months later.

Experience heightened awareness of mortality and well-being.

Discover the telltale sign of PTSD or a PTSD-like response - a phenomenon that renowned expert Dr. Bubrick refers to as an intense fixation on mortality or the absence of life. Introducing a fascinating paradox of childhood, where some children are drawn to the macabre, while others channel their focus into safeguarding their loved ones and ensuring their own safety. Are you constantly plagued by thoughts of potential disasters like open fires or catastrophic events?

Do you find yourself worrying about the safety of your own fireplace or the risk of earthquakes or floods in your area? It's time to put those concerns to rest and take control of your peace of mind.

Experience a transformation in your life with our revolutionary solution!

Say goodbye to issues with sleeping, eating, anger, and attention. Our cutting-edge approach is designed to address these challenges head-on, providing you with the relief and peace of mind you deserve. Don't let these obstacles hold you back any longer - take control of your well-being today!

Discover the striking resemblance between the symptoms of injury in children (and adults) and depressive disorder. From disrupted sleep patterns to fluctuating appetite, from unexplained irritability to difficulty concentrating on tasks and assignments, these shared signs can leave you wondering what's really going on. Experience the subtle yet powerful symptoms that may resemble anxiety attacks, as well as the overwhelming and persistent worry about separating from your parents.

Introducing: Triggers

One year following a heart-wrenching incident, it is only natural for us to reflect, evaluate, and honor the memory of those who were taken from us. Discover a multitude of anniversaries intertwined with the lives of children, as noted by the esteemed Dr. Bubrick. These anniversaries, such as the birthdays of departed friends or classmates, may unexpectedly impact them in profound ways. "Children can experience moments of uncertainty, but ultimately, they have the potential to thrive," he affirms. Introducing the incredible phenomenon: just a few moments away from the birthday, prepare to witness an abundance of symptoms. Experience the remarkable result.

Chapter 2

The Impact of Trauma in Childhood

However, grownups frequently remark things like, "He was so young when that happened." He won't even be able to remember it like an adult. Stress in childhood can have long-term effects. Children are resilient, but they're not indestructible.

That's not to imply that even if your child had a terrible experience, they will always be psychologically damaged. With the right approaches, adults may be able to assist children in better overcoming traumatic situations.

However, it's critical that you recognize when your child may require expert assistance in managing their stress. Early intervention could prevent your child from growing up with the trauma's aftereffects.

The Details:

- Various experiences may qualify as trauma. Abuse that is physical or intimate, for example, may clearly upset kids.

- One-time occurrences, such as car accidents or very severe natural disasters (like hurricanes), may also have a negative psychological impact on kids.

- Persistent stress, such as living in a dangerous neighborhood or experiencing bullying, can be traumatizing, even if it seems normal to an adult. Almost any experience might potentially be stressful for a child if: It happened ad hoc; It happened repeatedly; Someone was cruel purposely; The child was unprepared as a result.

- Childhood injuries don't always have to happen to the child; for instance, it can be quite upsetting to watch someone you care about suffer. Children who are exposed to violent media may also get traumatized.

- However, an encounter is not necessarily traumatic just because it is distressing. For example, parental divorce will probably have an impact on a child, although it doesn't always cause trauma.

- It's also critical to remember that just because a child has experienced a tragedy or a near-death event, traumatization is not a given. Compared to others, some children are significantly less affected by their diseases.

If it Causes PTSD

A lot of kids experience upsetting things at some point. Since the majority of them struggle to carry out a traumatic occurrence, most of them return to their regular employment status in a very short period of time.

Nevertheless, a large number of kids, typically three to fifteen percent of girls and one to six percent of males, experience post-traumatic stress disorder (PTSD).

Children suffering from PTSD could repeatedly feel the tension in their minds. They might also avoid situations that bring up the hurt, or they might use their enjoyment to act out their tension.

Children might think they missed clues that would have

indicated the terrible occurrence. In an attempt to avert such tragedies, they learn to be extremely watchful, constantly searching for signs that something horrible might occur.

Children suffering from post-traumatic stress disorder may also experience:

- Fear.
- Depression.
- Stress.
- Aggression and fury.
- Self-harming actions.
- Feelings of loneliness.
- Low self-worth.
- Having trouble placing others' faith.

In fact, even in the absence of PTSD, children may already display behavioral and psychological problems after going through a traumatic event. Following a distressing incident, keep the following in mind in the coming weeks:

- A greater concern for safety or death.
- Issues with resting.
- Modifications in hunger.
- Problems with anger.
- Distraction issues.
- Refusal at school.
- Somatic problems, such as stomachaches and headaches.
- A diminished desire to engage in daily activities.
- Sensitivity.
- Despondency.
- Emergence of fresh anxieties.
- Impact on Health in the Long Run.

- •The way a child's brain develops is altered by traumatic experiences, which can have long-term effects.

Research indicates that an individual's lifetime risk of health issues is positively correlated with the number of negative childhood experiences. The injury sustained in childhood may raise a person's chance of:

- Asthma.
- Depression.
- Disease of the cardiovascular system.
- The stroke.
- Diabetes.

Furthermore, a written article that appeared in Psychiatric Times in 2016 pointed out that people who had suffered trauma as children—such as physical or sexual abuse or parental domestic violence—were much more likely to have attempted suicide.

Impact on Interactions

A child's mental and physical well-being depends on his or her relationship with his or her caregiver, whether they be parents, grandparents, or someone else. The little one learns how to control their emotions, trust people, and connect with the outside world through this cooperation and connection.

It is exceedingly difficult for a child to build relationships throughout their early years, including with peers their own age, and into adulthood when they experience a personal injury that makes them believe they cannot trust or depend on that caregiver. Instead, the child is more likely to believe that the world is a scary place and that adults are dangerous.

Youngsters who fail to maintain strong relationships with their caregivers will probably have difficulty finding romantic partners when they get older. More than 21,000 Australian survivors of child abuse who were 60 years of age or older reported a higher than average percentage of failed partnerships.

How to lend assistance:

Support from the family may be essential to reducing the toll that stress takes on kids. Here are some strategies to support a child following a distressing experience:

- Encourage your child to discuss and get validation for his feelings.

- Answer inquiries truthfully.

- Assure your child that you'll take all reasonable precautions to keep him safe.

- As soon as you can, stick to your daily schedule in its entirety.

Consult your child's pediatrician if you've noticed behavioral or emotional changes in your child after she's experienced traumatic events. A physician can evaluate your child's health insurance and provide a referral for mental health services if necessary.

Your child may be eligible for therapies like family therapy, perform therapy, or cognitive behavioral therapy, depending on their needs and the generation they belong to. One further option for treating your child's symptoms could be medication.

Causes and Effects of Trauma on the Growth and Conduct of Children.

Internet Authorities MS Courses in Early Childhood Education The source explains how stress impacts a child's behavior and development and what early childhood educators need to know.

Graduates of programs at the early childhood education level will be equipped with the skills and knowledge necessary to identify the telltale signs of harm in children.

Children can face stress in a variety of ways, according to a counselor: natural catastrophes destroy communities, leaving families without a place to live. Shootings and attacks on the community often target children. Nonetheless, the most well-known psychological storms involve abuse and neglect that occur inside, where kids will most likely feel loved and safe. Even when grownups feel hurt, maturity allows them to deal with the days more effectively and return to a sense of normalcy.

Early-life experiences can actually change a child's developing brain, which can lead to behavioral and developmental issues.

Children who don't have strong relationships with their parents and other caretakers come to understand that they can't rely on others for assistance. Children who experience abuse and exploitation come to believe that they are flawed and that the world is dangerous and terrible. Trauma disrupts the body's stress response mechanisms, the normal development of the brain and nervous system, and the ability to fight off illness.

Find Out About Your Program

• *Signs of Trauma in Early Childhood*

When it comes to seeing, recognizing, and supporting young children who exhibit indicators of trauma in daycare, preschool, kindergarten, and elementary school environments, early childhood educators can be invaluable. It's critical that you recognize typical trauma symptoms, such as the following:

- Youngsters under the age of two frequently have inadequate speech skills.

- Display storage issues.

- Manifest an overly irritable mood.

- Excessively cry or scream.

- Display regressive behavior.

Children between the ages of three and six frequently: Develop learning impairments; Have difficulty learning or focusing in class.

☐ Use both constructive and destructive actions to draw attention.

Possess verbal abuse.

Headaches and stomachaches are experienced.

If early care and support are not provided, traumatized children grow up to be traumatized people who frequently exhibit aberrant stress reactions, long-term medical illnesses, interpersonal issues, learning disabilities, and propensities to engage in risky activities like drug misuse and breaking the law.

The Effects of Childhood Injury on the Mind

According to a recent study from the First Life Stress and Pediatric Anxiety Program at Stanford University School of Medicine, distressing stress has distinct effects on the developing brains of men and women.

The investigation discovered that there might be differences in the quantity and surface area of the insula between women and men who have experienced stressful stress and those who have not in young people exhibiting signs of post-traumatic stress disorder. Nestled deep inside the cerebral cortex, the insula plays a fundamental role in self-awareness, feelings, and interoceptive digestion—the degree to which an individual pays attention to sensory information in their torso. On January 9, the analysis made its online debut in the journal Depressive Disorder and Stress. This is the first study to look for sex differences in subdivisions from the insula in children who have experienced stress.

Strangely, not everyone who experiences trauma goes on to develop post-traumatic stress disorder (PTSD). People who are diagnosed with post-traumatic stress disorder (PTSD) or who have gone through a traumatic stress event in their lives are able to deal with real or perceived death as well as "intrusive" thoughts following the traumatic incident. These intrusive symptoms, which include dreams, flashbacks, and extreme, prolonged mental and physiological reactions as if the distressing event were still occurring (though it has long since stopped), are so called because the average person who experiences them finds them unpleasant and unwanted. As a result, the typical injured person who is susceptible to developing PTSD will avoid being reminded of the upsetting incident. They may also undergo cognitive and behavioral alterations, as well as persistently elevated arousal (APA, 2013). Prior studies in neuroscience have discovered that modifications in the insula following stress not only aid in the development of PTSD but also in its upkeep. Similarly, it had been discovered that women who sustain trauma would get PTSD (Hanson et al., 2008); however, researchers have not yet been able to determine why.

Fifty-nine young people, ranging in age from nine to seventeen, took part in the analysis. Of the individuals, half showed signs of PTSD, and the other half did not. The stress and non-trauma organizations shared comparable traits related to gender, IQ, and generation. Five of the thirty injured people (sixteen men and fourteen women) reported one upsetting stressor, whereas the other twenty-five (n=25) reported two or more upsetting stressors or chronic stress exposure. Experts used structural magnetic resonance imaging (SMRI) to scan each person's brain and compared the brains of healthy men and women to those of men and women suffering from post-traumatic stress disorder (PTSD). There were significant differences between men and women in the traumatized group, despite the fact that there were no structural differences in the insula subdivisions between the brains of healthy males and females. In contrast to the control group's teenagers, men with injuries had more insula amount and surface, whereas women under stress had lower insula quantity and surface. This discovery indicates that damage not only impacts the growing brain but also has distinct effects on the upbringing of children.

Insula volume decreases with age (Shaw et al., 2008), and the smaller amounts of insula in women with PTSD symptoms suggest that this area of the brain is aging faster than expected, which is partially explained by stressful stress. In their paper, Klabunde, Weems, Raman, & Carrion (2017) emphasized the importance of these findings, saying that "clinicians and scientists could probably develop sex-specific stress and emotion dysregulation treatments by better-understanding sex variations within a section of the mind associated with emotion control."

In addition, the approach sheds light on how character and nurture interact when evaluating intricate mental health conditions like PTSD. In addition to mental health professionals and patients understanding that environmental stress causes neurobiological changes that vary between the sexes, some people find it difficult to access tools like the MRI scanner used to interpret the study's findings. As a result, a one-size-fits-all approach to treating PTSD will be far less successful than a treatment that takes into account the circumstances of the average person, such as natural sex.

Chapter 3
How to Provide Comprehensive Rehab for Children.

Be aware that questions may continue: Children may occasionally have more questions due to the tragedy's aftermath, which includes continually shifting circumstances. Let them know you're available to talk at any time. Kids must analyze information on their own, follow a schedule, and ask questions when they don't know what to ask.

Encourage your family to talk about the increasing death of a loved one. Children are more willing to talk about their emotions when they can talk and share their sorrows as a family.

Generally speaking, avoid giving kids too much responsibility: It's important to avoid giving kids adult-level responsibilities or overloading them with work because that will be too stressful for them. Rather, you should gradually reduce your expectations for school and domestic duties, even though it's still a good idea to complete some of these chores.

Children with special needs should receive extra attention because they can require more time, care, and support than other kids. You may make your vocabulary simpler and use it more often. It can be necessary to adapt information to your child's level of understanding; for instance, a child with a language handicap might benefit more from the use of visual aids or other common forms of communication.

Keep an eye out for signs of trauma: It's very normal for youngsters to appear to be doing fine during the first month following a disaster. After that, the numbness wears off, and children may suffer more symptoms. This is especially the case for children who have lost close family members, witnessed accidents or fatalities, had already faced stress in their lives, or have not been placed in a new household.

Know when to seek help: Although stress and other problems can linger for weeks, if they don't go away or your child begins to hear voices, see things that aren't there, become paranoid, experience panic attacks, or express thoughts of wanting to harm himself or others, get help right away from a mental health professional or your loved ones' doctor.

Taking care of yourself will allow you to assist your child in the greatest way possible. Talk about your worries with your friends and family; you could even form a sort of support group. Participate in church or community group activities as usual; make an effort to eat healthfully, stay hydrated, follow workout regimens, and obtain adequate sleep. Psychological susceptibility is mitigated by physical well-being. Breathe like a yogi to relieve stress. If your extreme anxiety is interfering with your capacity to function, see a medical professional or mental health professional; if you are unable to find one, see a religious leader. Acknowledge that you need assistance and obtain it. If not for any other reason, behave in your child's best interest.

How to Help Kids in the 0–2 Age Range

Your son or daughter will feel safe and secure if you remain calm, as babies pick up on your emotions and respond accordingly. When a child experiences stress and overwhelm, they may react by fussing, having difficulty being calmed down, eating or sleeping irregularly, or withdrawing from their job.

Make an effort to engage in a relaxing activity. Take hold of your infant and speak calmly to them even if you are feeling pressed for time or worried.

Attend to your baby's needs on a regular basis. Typically, the age group's developmental task is to trust caregivers in order to help children form a positive, healthy bond.

After you have been nursing, keep nursing. It is untrue, despite the misconception that if a mother experiences stress, her breast milk deteriorates and the baby may become "sluggish" or develop learning difficulties. It is essential to maintain your child's health and relationship with you by having regular checkups. It's important for you to maintain your health in order to breastfeed, so make sure you consume enough water.

Consider your child's eye, give them a smile, and give them a touch. Studies reveal that touch, vision contact, and being in a mother's presence all contribute to a baby's emotional equilibrium.

Ways to Assist Children in Generations 2–5

At this age, children still require parental care even if they are making great developmental advancements. They usually react to events according to way their parents do, much like babies do. When you are confident and at ease, your child will benefit from it more. If you appear anxious or overburdened, your child can feel in danger.

Children between the ages of two and five typically react as follows:

- Discussing the role or acting as though you are "playing" it frequently.

- Tarts or agitated outbursts.

- Weeping and being emotional.

- Enhanced dread, frequently stemming from the dark, creatures, or alone.

- Enhanced awareness of external stimuli such as wind, thunder, and other sounds.

- Disturbances in sleeping, eating, and using the restroom.

- wishing that this disaster could be reversed.

- Extreme difficulty parting and clinging to caretakers.

- Going back to infantile habits such as bedwetting, thumb-sucking, and baby talk.

Your Ability:

Keep your child secure by giving them hugs and cuddles whenever you can. Tell her you'll take care of her if she's upset or scared. When teaching young children to speak, start with basic expressions like "Mommy's here."

Be careful what you say because young children have large ears and may be able to pick up on your anxiety, misunderstand what they hear, or become unduly afraid of things they don't fully grasp.

Maintain routines wherever you can: Try your best to adhere to normal bedtimes and mealtimes, regardless of your living circumstances. Make new routines if you've moved or are homeless. When everyone goes to bed, try to complete the rituals you have always done with your children, such singing songs or saying prayers.

Provide additional support before bedtime: Children who have experienced trauma may have anxiety at night. Spend more time than usual discussing or reading bedtime stories to your child. It's acceptable to set up a temporary sleeping arrangement for young children to spend the night with you, but make sure the data they can access allows them to schedule a regular time to go to bed.

Keep youngsters away from the news: Young children may mix up facts and worries. They were unable to discern that the scenes they saw on the news are not recurring. They also don't have to pay attention to the radio.

Encourage kids to talk about their emotions by asking them basic questions like, "How are you feeling today? To make kids feel much better and more at ease, participate in family activities or read aloud from a favorite story during any conversations regarding the previous incident.

Give your child the freedom to narrate the events of the story; this will help them feel more at ease and manage their feelings. Having fun can frequently be a terrific way to help your child explain the story's narrative and function in her own terms.

Make drawings: Young children typically find success in using drawings to convey their emotions. That gives you another opportunity to reassure and explain. You could remark on something a child has drawn attention to, for example, to start a conversation.

If your child misbehaves, it may be a sign that she needs more care. Assist her in identifying her feelings, such as fear. Furious? Depressing? Show her the proper way to behave after reassuring her that it is okay to trust her in that way. You can say something like, "It's okay to get upset, but it probably isn't okay to your sister."

Get youngsters involved in activities: For children in this age range, distraction is a great thing. Play enjoyable video games with them and ask to play with other children.

Talk about what's going well: In fact, during what are likely the most trying times, it's critical that you acknowledge and share positive developments in order to support your child's recovery in the long run. Saying something like, "We nonetheless experience each other," is one possibility. Making a point of being kind to others could also make you feel better. I'm here for you, and I'll stand by you.

How to help children between the ages of two and five deal with the growing death of a loved one:

Speak to them on their level: Use analogies, such as the dog's death or changes in the plants in your yard, to help them comprehend concepts.

Give brief explanations, such as "When someone passes away, we can't find them anymore, but we can still look at them in pictures; please remember them."

Reassure your kids: They might believe that what happened is their fault; let them know that's not the case.

Anticipate more questions: This is how young children absorb knowledge.

How to Help Kids between the Ages of 6 to 11

Children at this age can talk about their feelings and ideas more easily and may be able to handle challenges better, but they still look to their parents for support and comfort. For any scared child, hearing them shows that you are dedicated to helping them throughout scary situations could be the most comforting thing.

Children between the ages of six and eleven typically react as follows:

- Fear and Uncertainty.

- Enhanced hostility, rage, and impatience (such as peer bullying or fights).

- Unrest in terms of appetite and sleep.

- Holding oneself responsible for the event.

- Sultry or sobbing.

- Fears about not being well taken care of.

- Fear for the family's lives or potential harm in the future.

- Denying that the function even took place

- Physical discomfort issues resulting from stress, including headaches, tiredness, and stomach aches

- Asking lots of questions

Refusing to discuss the purpose (more common in children aged 9 to 11)

Retraction from social engagements

Educational issues: Difficulties with recall and focus in class, unwillingness to back down.

Your ability to be of considerable assistance;

Assure your child that they are secure by using facts to reassure them. Use genuine phrases like hurricane, earthquake, overflow, and aftershock. Knowledge empowers the generation's youth and reduces stress and worry.

Maintain as much "normalcy" as you can: mealtime and bedtime rituals provide children a sense of security. If you are homeless or have already moved, establish new routines and give your child some control over the situation. Allowing your child to choose the story to watch before bed, for example, gives them a sense of control during a confusing period.

Limit your child's exposure to TV, newspapers, and radio: school-age children will get more concerned the more false information they encounter. Information and video can exacerbate the stress caused by the function, so whenever a youngster watches an informational program or concentrates on the radio, take a seat with them so you can talk about it later. Don't let your child access visual media.

Spend time conversing with your child to teach him or her that it's okay to express worries and ask inquiries. Using family time (such mealtimes) to discuss family and local news is one way to promote conversation among family members. Additionally, find out what his buddies have previously said so you can rectify any inaccuracies.

Briefly but honestly respond to questions: When a child offers to talk about something, get his opinions first so you can determine exactly what the issue is. Children typically ask questions when they are concerned about a particular issue. Provide a comforting response. It's actually acceptable to say, "I don't know," unless you have knowledge of the answer to a question. Generally speaking, avoid speculating or acting on hearsay.

Get kids who don't talk much: Start a dialogue by expressing your emotions; for example, you could say, "That's a really scary thing, and sometimes I wake up in the middle of the night because I'm thinking a lot." What state are you in?". By doing this, you can help your child know that they are not alone in their worries. But generally speaking, don't go into great detail about your fears.

Keep them busy: Routines like visiting friends or attending school might have been disturbed. Assist children in considering alternative activities and setting up playgroups with other parents.

Calm concerns about friends' safety: Tell your kids that their friends' parents are watching out for them, since you might be watching out for them as well.

Talk about community recovery. If necessary, let kids know that efforts are being made to keep them safe or that normal water and electricity are being restored with help from local organizations and government agencies.

Encourage children to assist: If they appear helpless, this will give them a feeling of accomplishment and purpose at the same time. Little ones can help you out with personal chores, and older ones can help out with volunteer work in the community.

Find similar: In order to extract, children must begin to perceive the future. This generation of children values details. In the event of natural disaster, for instance, you may state: "People are sending food, medicine, and regular water from coast to coast." They have constructed new facilities for the study and care of injured people, and they plan to construct new residences. Things are rather challenging for the time being.

How to help children between the ages of 6 and 11 deal with the growing number of deaths

Find out what your youngster is thinking about by asking questions before assuming to know what your child genuinely wants to know. You could say, for instance, "I was really saddened by grandma's passing." Consider yourself. It's challenging to consider, isn't it?"

School-age children tend to be puzzled by vague responses, therefore use genuine terms instead of euphemisms for lack of real life, such as "He visited a far greater place." Alternatively, you may explain, "Grandma has passed away; she will not be coming back. It's okay to feel sad about this."

Become as honest as you can by using basic illustrations to explain things like your body and accidents.

Tell your child that feelings like anger and grief are normal and that if she suppresses them, it could make her feel much worse in the future.

Assemble your offspring for impending adjustments to daily schedules or domestic duties. Talk about what the real changes entail for him/her.

Assure your child: Help them understand that having problems with classmates, family, and college is common and acceptable at this time.

Promote thoughtful memorializing by leading a family in prayer and escorting your child to the Chapel to light a candle. It might also be necessary for your child to write a note to the departed or draw a picture before you hang up.

Show patience: Children up to generation eleven may find it difficult to accept that the average person might not return and may believe that the rising death toll is changeable. You may find yourself saying things like, "I'm sad because he died, and he's not coming back."

How to help kids for a very long time (12–18 years)

For teenagers, adolescence was already difficult since their bodies were going through so many changes. They struggle to ask their parents for greater independence, and they also have a tendency to believe that very little can go wrong. Unsettling incidents may give the impression that they are out of control, even if they are strong. They will also feel bad for the people who are going through the tragedy, and they have a strong desire to know why the function happened.

Children's typical responses, ranging from 12 to 18:

- Steer clear of emotions.

- Constantly thinking back on the catastrophe.

- Releasing themselves from friends and relatives.

- Discontent or hostility.

- Suicidal thoughts and depression together.

- Excessive worry, including concerns about the future.

- Feel erratic and easily agitated.

- Changes in sleeping and/or eating patterns.

- Academic problems, include difficulty focusing and remembering things, as well as a refusal to back down in the classroom.

- Engaging in hazardous or illegal activities, such as consuming alcohol

Your aptitude;

Restore your child's sense of safety: Kids find it quite compelling to display their vulnerability; they may try to pretend that everything is alright even when it's not. Even if they could resist hugs, your touch could make them feel safe. You may say something like, "I know you're produced now, but I just need to give you a hug."

Encourage teenagers to feel useful by giving them little tasks and household responsibilities, then praising them for their accomplishments and self-handling.

Teenagers should typically not be overburdened with obligations, especially ones that seem adult-like, as this could make them more anxious.

Let the conversation begin: Teenagers frequently express that they would prefer not to talk. If you are working together on a task, try to strike up a chat so that the topic won't grow too heated or contentious.

Think about creating a peer organization. Some teenagers may find it easier to communicate in groups with their peers. Encourage conversation with other well-respected adults as well, such as your instructor or relatives.

Reduce your exposure to radio, newspapers, and television: Teens are more able to handle the news than younger children, but those who find it difficult to cut off their connection to these media may be trying to use them as a detrimental coping mechanism for their anxiety. In any case, have a conversation with your child about what he or she has observed or noticed.

Encourage your child to take initiative: Children in that age range want to assist the town. Find suitable volunteer positions.

Recognize drug abuse: Adolescents are especially vulnerable to using drugs or alcohol as a stress reliever. Consult a doctor if your child behaves strangely or if they seem to be under the influence of alcohol or drugs. and grasp your offspring in a somewhat intimate manner. For instance, following a catastrophe, people frequently turn to alcohol or drugs as a way to cope or forget, but doing so might exacerbate existing issues. Other things you may do include go on a stroll, share your hopes and dreams for a better future, or discuss how you're feeling with friends and family.

How to help children aged 12 to 18 deal with the growing number of deaths

Be patient: It's possible that teenagers struggle to communicate their feelings regarding dying. Start a conversation starter by saying something along the lines of, "I know it's awful that granny died away. According to experts, talking about our feelings makes sense. How are things going for you?"

Become extremely honest: Talk about your feelings; the rising death rate may be affecting their actions.

Be adaptable: At this point, it's acceptable to have some more latitude when it comes to rules, behavioral goals, and educational objectives.

Remember in a meaningful way by letting your children light a candle in the cathedral and praying together at home. You will have to include him/her in memorial services; in addition, he/she might like having a private family remembrance performed at home.

What Teachers Can Do to Help Students a Lot

As soon as you can, get back into the routine: Kids tend to perform better when they know what to expect. Having a regular school period may assist youngsters believe that the upsetting events do not govern their entire daily lives. Stay up to date with the students' goals.

It doesn't have to be perfect, but having homework assignments and basic classwork to do has become beneficial.

Be aware of the warning signals that a child may require more support: Students who are unable to function due to intense feelings of despair, anxiety, or rage should be sent to a mental health professional. Stress in children can sometimes take the form of physical ailments like headaches, stomachaches, or severe tiredness.

Encourage children to comprehend the events better by, for instance, outlining the various forms of assistance that are available and offering constructive coping mechanisms.

Examine a memorial: memorials are typically a fantastic place to remember those who have lost loved ones or items. College memorials should be brief, pertinent to the needs of the entire campus community, and lasting many hours. Youngsters less than four may not have the eye span necessary to be included. a well-known friend, caregiver, or child participating in comparative medicine at memorial or burial ceremonies.

Children's fears decrease when they realize that responsible people are taking the necessary precautions to ensure their safety. Assure them that college officials are working to ensure their safety.

Keep in contact with parents: Inform them about events and programs offered by the school so they are prepared for any discussions to take place at home. Parents should be urged to restrict their kids' exposure to news articles.

It's possible that you are too involved in helping your students to give yourself enough attention. Look for ways that you and your coworkers can support one another.

Indications of harm in children and teenagers

- o Replaying the function in their heads on a regular basis.
- o Fears at night.
- o Thinks that most of the world is dangerous.
- o Moodiness, irritability, and rage.

- Insufficient focus.
- Issues with rest or appetite.
- Problematic behavior.
- Fear of someone approaching too closely.
- Vexation due to loud noises
- Small children reverting to earlier behaviors, like clinging, bedwetting, or thumb-sucking
- A hard time falling asleep.
- Distancing or retreating from other people.
- Encourage teens to use drugs or alcohol.
- Functional impairment: Not being able to learn, play with friends, attend school, etc.

Chapter 4

Discover the Essential Guide to Caring for Traumatized Children.

Discover the power of effectively managing children during traumatic encounters to proactively avoid future challenges.

Discover the profound influence that a connection with traumatic events can have on the lives of children.

Discover the wide range of challenges that children across the globe may face, from physical and emotional abuse during their formative years to enduring the aftermath of natural disasters or political turmoil. These resilient young souls may also bear witness to a multitude of violent events, leaving an indelible mark on their tender hearts and minds. The emotional toll of such stress on children is as diverse as the experiences themselves. Discover the fascinating world of injury response, where subjectivity reigns supreme. Witness the myriad of methods through which young minds can react to the harrowing experience of trauma. Discover the key factors that influence a child's response to strain:

Experience the transformative power of this remarkable tie that has weathered a traumatic event. Whether it's a brief encounter or a prolonged exposure, rest assured that its enduring effects are far-reaching. Experience the raw intensity of a traumatic event, whether it be the harrowing ordeal of extreme physical assault or the haunting specter of witnessing a sexual assault. Unlock a world of support resources that cater to your child's needs, be it through the warmth of informal assistance or the expertise of formal public support services.

Discover the astonishing resilience of children who bravely face traumatic events, seemingly unscathed. However, it's crucial to acknowledge that for certain children, the aftermath can be far-reaching and profound. These resilient young souls may experience a range of long-term consequences, such as the emergence of psychological challenges, physical ailments, and even the risk of substance abuse, personality disorders, depression, or the unthinkable tragedy of suicide.

Discover the alarming truth: traumatized children are at risk of developing a full-blown posttraumatic stress disorder. But that's not all - brace yourself for the latest revelation from the Diagnostic and Statistical Manual of Mental Disorders. Prepare for the introduction of a groundbreaking diagnosis called Developmental Trauma Disorder (DTD). This cutting-edge diagnosis is specifically designed for children who endure repeated traumas while their young minds are still in the crucial stages of development. Introducing the highly recommended requirements for DTD:

- Introducing the power of publicity! Experience the impact of multiple or chronic contacts with various types of adverse developmental traumas.

- Introducing the remarkable phenomenon of triggered dysregulation! Prepare to be amazed as your emotions, body, and behaviors respond in unique and fascinating ways to specific situational triggers. Brace yourself for a rollercoaster of affective, somatic, and behavioral patterns that will leave you breathless!

- Introducing: Persistently Altered Attributions and Expectancies! Introducing the all-new solution to your trust-related concerns! Say goodbye to insufficient trust protectors, negative self-attitude, and the perception that future victimization is inevitable. Experience a life free from practical impairments with our revolutionary approach. Experience challenges in education, family, law, or career.

- Discover the undeniable importance of conducting a specialized analysis on childhood trauma. Countless years of extensive research have unequivocally demonstrated the pervasive prevalence of trauma among teenagers. Discover the shocking findings of a groundbreaking 2002 study that interviewed 1,420 children. Prepare to be astounded as you learn that a staggering one in four adolescent children have endured the unimaginable - extreme stressors such as abuse and other traumatic events. These distressing experiences have left an indelible mark on their young lives. Discover the shocking truth: a staggering eighteen percent of young individuals have reported experiencing multiple stressors. But here's the real eye-opener: our expert analysts have uncovered a fascinating connection. It turns out that exposure to just one extreme stressor significantly increases the likelihood of encountering even more stressors over time. Brace yourself for the impact of this groundbreaking discovery! Discover the undeniable evidence from additional studies that confirms the urgent need for immediate treatment in children who have suffered injuries. Act swiftly to prevent or minimize long-term damage.

Discover the ultimate solution for childhood trauma - the most reliable treatment awaits! Discover the groundbreaking insights in the latest article from Canadian Mindset, where a comprehensive overview of cutting-edge treatments for children who have experienced trauma awaits. Dive into the world of innovative therapies designed to heal and empower young minds. Introducing a groundbreaking article brought to you by a team of esteemed psychologists from the prestigious University of English Columbia and Kelowna's renowned Youngsters Forensic Psychiatric Services. This enlightening piece sheds light on the current state of research surrounding the efficacy of various treatment plans for addressing adolescent stress. It reveals a startling truth - the extent of research in this area pales in comparison to the vast body of knowledge available for treating traumatized adults. Brace yourself for a thought-provoking exploration into the world of adolescent stress management.

Discover the undeniable power of cognitive-behavioral therapies (CBT), the top choice among therapists. With extensive research backing its effectiveness, CBT outshines psychoanalytic or medication-based treatments. Experience the transformative potential of CBT today. Introducing a groundbreaking approach, CBT was initially designed to address injuries in adults. However, recognizing the unique needs of adolescent stress patients, a modified treatment option has emerged, specifically tailored to children. This innovative approach places children at the forefront, ensuring their well-being is prioritized. Introducing a range of cutting-edge treatment options for your needs, including the revolutionary Multi-Modality Trauma Treatment (MMTT). With its origins dating back to 1998, MMTT has been at the forefront of trauma therapy, providing unparalleled results. Introducing MMTT, a revolutionary approach that recognizes the impact of stress on the development of children. Our cutting-edge techniques, rooted in age-appropriate Cognitive Behavioral Therapy (CBT), are designed to empower children to effectively navigate through traumatic experiences. Introducing the remarkable MMTT programs! Designed for college settings, these programs offer a comprehensive 14-program format. Experience a range of transformative activities including psychoeducation, narrative writing to express your distressing experiences, effective publicity and relaxation techniques, and cognitive restructuring. Unleash your potential with MMTT! Discover the remarkable findings of empirical studies on MMTT, showcasing its ability to significantly reduce stress symptoms. Not only that, but it also demonstrates promising results in alleviating symptoms of major depression, anger, and anxiousness. Experience the transformative power of MMTT today!

Discover the remarkable benefits of MMTT, a groundbreaking program meticulously designed to cater to the unique needs of traumatized children. Unlike other programs, MMTT focuses on children who have encountered a single traumatic event, ensuring tailored support and effective healing. Discover the untapped potential of MMTT in managing polytrauma cases, a field that is still ripe for exploration.

Introducing Trauma-Focused Cognitive Behavioral Therapy (TF-CBT) - a groundbreaking approach pioneered in 2006 by the esteemed Judith Cohen and her esteemed colleagues. Introducing TF-CBT, the groundbreaking therapy designed exclusively for children aged three to eighteen.

Discover the transformative power of TF-CBT treatment programs, carefully designed to provide your child with the support they need. With a range of eight to twenty classes, these programs offer a unique opportunity for your child to grow and heal, either on their own or alongside a loving parent or caregiver. Experience the positive impact of TF-CBT today. Introducing TF-CBT: Empowering Children to Conquer Traumatic Memories Introducing the revolutionary component-based mode: TF-CBT! This structured approach is designed to bring you results, all thanks to the powerful acronym "PRACTICE." Get ready to unlock your full potential! Experience the transformative power of treatment for children. Our expert therapists provide a comprehensive approach that includes psychoeducation, training in rest skills, effective appearance and modulation techniques, and cognitive coping skills. Give your child the tools they need to thrive and succeed. Enroll them in our exceptional treatment program today. Discover the incredible power of injury narration and cognitive processing for children. Experience the transformative effects of in vivo connection with master injury reminders. Unleash the potential of conjoint mother or father-child sessions to foster growth and safety. Don't miss out on this opportunity to motivate and enhance your child's well-being. Originally designed to assist individuals affected by intimate mistreatment, TF-CBT has proven its effectiveness in addressing various forms of trauma and has become widely utilized in treatment settings worldwide.

Introducing Stanford Cue-Centered Therapy (SCCT) - a groundbreaking approach developed by the esteemed researchers at Stanford College of Medicine's Early Life Stress Research Program. Introducing SCCT, the ultimate short-term treatment approach that focuses on providing personalized therapy for children and equipping them with the necessary tools to overcome trauma. Discover the power of SCCT and unlock your child's potential for healing. Introducing SCCT - the ultimate solution for addressing a child's cognitive, affective, behavioral, and physical challenges. With its cutting-edge cognitive-behavioral techniques, rest training, narrative utilization, and top-notch parental training, SCCT is designed to provide comprehensive support and treatment. Introducing SCCT, the revolutionary solution designed to diminish your child's negative thoughts and cognitive patterns, while also reducing their sensitivity to distressing memories. Say goodbye to mental burdens and hello to a brighter future! Introducing SCCT - the ultimate program designed to empower children with essential coping skills. With a duration of fifteen to eighteen classes, SCCT stimulates young minds to embrace the power of rest and self-empowerment. Say goodbye to stress and hello to a brighter future with SCCT! Empower children to understand the impact of trauma on their lives, enabling them to take charge of their reactions when faced with distressing reminders.

Introducing SCCT: The Ultimate Solution with a Guarantee! Experience the Power of SCCT: Transforming Lives One Therapy Session at a Time! Discover the Revolutionary SCCT: Unleash Your Potential with Personalized Therapy! Unlock Your True Potential with SCCT: Overcome Frustration and Embrace Success! Discover the untapped potential of SCCT with our groundbreaking case studies.

Introducing Seeking Security - a groundbreaking program initially designed to address substance abuse and trauma in both adults and adolescents. Discover the five essential pillars of Seeking Protection: prioritizing personal safety, seamlessly integrating trauma and substance abuse support, tailoring the approach to the client's unique needs, emphasizing the treatment process, and honing in on cognitions, behaviors, interpersonal interactions, and case management. Experience a comprehensive and holistic approach to protection like never before. Introducing Seeking Security - the ultimate solution tailored exclusively for children. This groundbreaking treatment model incorporates the power of psychoeducation, specialized coping skills training, and cognitive restructuring techniques. Say goodbye to worries and hello to a brighter future with Seeking Security. Experience the power of parental participation in the revolutionary Seeking Safeness program. Unlock the potential for a safer future for your family. Discover the convenience and accessibility of our online training programs. Take the first step towards a brighter tomorrow.

Introducing Trauma Affect Rules: Your go-to resource for Education and Therapy (with a focus on) - Originally crafted and rigorously tested with young offenders in mind. Unlock your full potential with Focus, the versatile solution that can be tailored to your needs. Whether you prefer the personal touch of individual sessions or the dynamic energy of group classes, Focus has you covered. Experience the power of focused learning and achieve your goals like never before. Choose Focus today! Discover the transformative power of Target. Our mission is to empower clients with a deep understanding of how trauma affects the brain's stress response, while equipping them with the tools to master their mindset and find solace in the face of adversity. Introducing the revolutionary prospective model, designed to empower you with the Independence acronym. With its powerful steps - concentrate, recognize triggers, feeling self-check, assess thoughts, define goals, options, and contribute - this model will guide you towards success and self-fulfillment. Say goodbye to confusion and hello to clarity with the Independence acronym. Discover the remarkable benefits of Concentrate on, a revolutionary approach similar to TF-CBT. One of its standout features is that parents are not burdened with the complexities of treatment. Experience the freedom and ease of Concentrate on today! Discover the cutting-edge empirical research on TARGET's value, focusing on the fascinating world of young offenders.

Four Ways to Begin Healing from Trauma During Childhood.

When Bill was six years old, his mother unexpectedly passed away from an aneurysm. When Teresa was ten years old, she was hit by a car and spent several months in a hospital, scared and frequently alone with no family support. Oliver never saw his father again after his parents got divorced when he was twelve years old. Trauma; the unforeseen catastrophe that explodes your lifestyle; a lack of vitality. a sad incident. Following an event, one may experience physical discomfort, anxiety, and sadness itself, in addition to struggling to make sense of what happened.

Adults undoubtedly deal with the same issue, but

children manage it in a different way due to their disability. They do not have this adult's whole functioning, logical brain. Their worldview is naturally narrow-minded and self-serving, and they have few coping mechanisms. When asked why their parents were divorced, one eight-year-old I spoke with said right away that it was because one night they forgot to shut down their research. Oliver and Teresa will probably have similar experiences.

Whatever "this" may be—abandonment, suffering, fear, or a lack of control—a child makes an unconscious or semi-conscious choice about what they must do to prevent it from happening again.

The most popular choices are as follows:

"*I take care of myself*"

The world is dangerous. I take care of myself, I can't trust anyone else, and I am myself. I'm unbiased; some may even say independent. I don't start and let people in; I don't slim down into human interactions. Instead, if you're reasonable and flexible, I oversee others.

"I'm compliant and passive."

The world is not safe. Personally, I think my lack of control comes from my high level of confidence in myself. I so concluded that I must choose others. They are wiser than I am, and occasionally they give me advice or support when I'm feeling overwhelmed.

"I need to stay vigilant."

The world is dangerous, therefore I have to live on edge all the time. I'm constantly worried, on the lookout for danger, and bracing myself for the worse. A friend is running late? He was in an automobile accident once. Why hasn't my partner phoned me today? He is considering divorcing. People may mistakenly think that I'm easily irritated or perpetually tense, even when I actually am.

"I must maintain control, when I'm angry."

Nothing is likely to elude me since the world is dangerous. Since I'm in command, almost little happens until I give the order. Do people bother me? I struggle. If you don't agree, you will quickly learn about it.

These positions, chiseled from suffering, become entrenched. They are effective because they give the child the freedom to succeed in life and get by during their formative years. They persist and spread, which is the issue. Even after getting married, a person may never truly feel intimate with their spouse. Their inaction keeps people from discovering their own lives in addition to driving them insane. Their anxiety helps them survive over the long run, but they also struggle with the world and lack control because of their negativity overshadowing the positive, their overreactions interfering with their interactions, or their dominance of their rage.

Being less fearful and more adaptable is the aim. Change occurs at multiple stages:

1. Start by acknowledging your predicament and critically examining its constraints.

What is your desired worldview and approach to caring for others? In doing so, you begin to separate the past from the present even though you are only being honest with yourself.

2. Obtain resolution.

By trying to bring things to a close and expressing what you were unable to say throughout those days, you wish to start healing some of the wounds. Try drafting a letter to someone—in Bill's instance, his mother; Teresa, the drivers of the cars; Oliver, his parents; or just her family, who wasn't always there. Write all you can't say at the time. Then, have them send you another note expressing what you truly want to hear—that they may be sorry, that it wasn't your fault, and that they loved you. Give your characters as much detail as you can, and feel free to write about everything that comes to mind.

3. Vary from your routines and comfort zones.

Time and effort to become the mature adult rather than the terrified child. Take a step outside of your safe haven and try speaking up instead of remaining passive, focusing on the here and now rather than dwelling on the terrible possibilities all the time, or letting go of control and anger.

4. Seek assistance and support.

Naturally, it's easier said than done, because support and assistance are just things you never truly got. Here, you can use the chance to get expert assistance in order to support and create those baby steps towards changing your behavior. You can also, on the recommendation of your therapist, think about taking medication to help break the pattern. things's more important to experience things in a new way than to convey it completely.

Chapter 5

Caring for Children Who Have Experienced Trauma

1. Recognize the Differences Between Feelings and Actions:

People are not more likely to be able to regulate their emotions, especially children. It is indeed "acceptable" to feel irate, irritated, or hurt. It is genuinely "acceptable" to feel driven to take action when experiencing despair or insanity. Kids can manage their conduct, but they still need to find out.

They require assistance telling emotions from actions. They might get help with this if they are taught constructive self-talk. By encouraging self-talk, you not only help children act responsibly but also affirm their feelings.

Examples: "I know you're upset; if someone had said something hurtful to me, I would be upset too." But you don't have to act cruelly once more. Make a suggestion to them about your strength.

"Even though most of us don't always look good, it's still important to treat others with respect."

2. Try to be as consistent as you can and use the 1-2-3 discipline method:

- Make a carefully worded request for the child's achievement.

- Reiterate your demand and warn them of the consequences if they do not comply.

- Provide the outcome. It seems sense to offer a consequence linked to the action, or what therapists refer to as a "natural" outcome. For instance, they shouldn't watch TV until after finishing their study or tidying their room.

But it's also crucial to never put a child in a situation from which they are unable to recover, like turning off the TV for extended periods of time. In particular, it's usually preferable to begin each day with a fresh start for younger, preteen kids.

3. Give kids a variety of coping mechanisms to learn:

Children frequently don't know that there's another way to entirely eliminate negative emotions than blowing out. Assist in teaching them that there are other paths to happiness that won't lead to more issues (such as returning the favor by acting inappropriately, hurting another person, or breaking something they value by throwing it in a fit of rage or mental distress).

Good coping strategy types include:

- See a friend or teacher who can offer support. Think of an activity you enjoy doing. Create a graphic or play a game.

  - Inhale deeply ten times, then think of something that makes you joyful.
  - Workout

4. Develop Empathy

This is sometimes referred to as "psychological cunning"

or "interpersonal and psychological learning" (SEL). Kids frequently require assistance in comprehending the idea of putting themselves in another person's shoes. You can help kids develop trust on how precisely someone else will be perceived by using role-playing games or other similar video games. These will remain your switch functions for role-playing. You can also read them stories about other kids and ask them to believe the feelings of the kids in the narrative.

Perhaps it would be beneficial to focus on teaching children the distinctions between different types of emotions. These activities can be carried out in a classroom or any other designated group setting, but they can't focus on any one student specifically.

Ways to Support a Traumatized Child in an Educational Setting.

Some of our students have disastrous outcomes as a result of chronic stress. How exactly can educators assist?

According to the Children's Defense Account, one in six

Latino men and one in three African American children born in 2001 will end up behind bars at some point in their lives. These astounding numbers are unfathomably awful. But in order to make them better, we need to adjust the way we view the children who are hidden behind the numbers.

Joyce, who is among us, assists administrators and teachers in just this manner. Through her award-winning UCSF Healthy Conditions and Response to Stress in universities (HEARTS) program, Joyce collaborates with the Scholar, Family, Community Support Division of the San Francisco Bay Area Unified College District and numerous underprivileged San Francisco Bay Area universities. Joyce truly helps teachers see that a misbehaving child is typically a scared youngster, even if teachers sometimes approach them as an unhealthy, rude, or defiant child. Put simply, a chronic connection to traumatic events outside of the child's control may be the cause of the child's conduct.

In addition to altering behavior, trauma can seriously impair a student's capacity to learn. It is evident to researchers that children who experience trauma on a regular basis develop additional social, mental, cognitive, and natural problems. These problems include difficulty controlling their emotions, taking care of themselves, and forming healthy relationships, all of which make it extremely difficult for a child to succeed in school.

However, trauma exposure does not guarantee one's fate. There are things that educators and other caring adults can do to lessen the effects of trauma and support students in thriving rather than failing, as the UCSF HEARTS program demonstrates.

The Danger of Complicated Traumas

The majority of us have gone through some kind of traumatic event at some point in our lives, whenever a circumstance became too much for our bodies or minds to handle. Based on our internal and external resources, a good number of people were most likely able to get better. However, after enduring what is known as complex stress, children who live in underserved neighbourhoods where racial discrimination, home and neighbourhood assault, and poverty are more common can develop post-trauma issues.

Complex damage is the result of ongoing exposure to traumatic events on a regular basis, almost all of which take place while a caregiver is present. When a kid is unable to rely on a close caregiver for security and comfort, either because of the caregiver's psychological difficulties or because the caregiver may have been the source of trauma, the child's ability to process and recover from harmful stress is severely compromised.

In her educational setting, Joyce compares the effects of complicated trauma to a vinyl record. A groove is carved into the record each time a track is played repeatedly; should someone accidentally bump the record player while another track is being played, the needle will miss the mark and fall into the deepest groove, reproducing the previous track. Sometimes, as you get to the last note of the song, the groove is so deep that the needle skips back to play it again.

Complex trauma leaves a groove in your brain, just like a

needle with an archival player does. Therefore, when a non-threatening event occurs that triggers memories of the traumatic incident, our bodies relive the uncomfortable response, preparing us to flee or confront the danger while deactivating other cognitive and rational processes. If this keeps happening, it will be simpler to trigger the fear reaction, which prevents our bodies from recovering. When we remove the context of trauma from our conduct, it may seem irrational or harsh after a while as we grow accustomed to this constant triggering.

A child in a school may enter into this routine by the teacher just raising his or her voice to gain everyone's attention or by unintentionally bumping into another student. When a child is induced, their irrational psychological and occasionally bodily reaction often makes no sense at all to the teacher, making it challenging for the teacher to react appropriately.

Methods for Teachers to Use

What specifically can educators do to support children in their classes who have suffered from biological trauma?

Joyce provides her teachers with the following four techniques.

1) Acknowledge that a child will engage in goal-setting and react in a considerate, caring manner. When you visit a youngster who may be struggling, start by asking yourself, "What's going on here?" rather than, "What's wrong with this child?" This small shift in perspective may assist you in realizing that the faculty student is still in a state of fear and anxiety, which can manifest in a variety of ways. The student could, for instance:

- Get a "deer-in-the-headlights" expression.

- Turn red and ball their hands.

- Inhale more quickly.

- Starting to move as their body prepares to run or respond.

- Tear up or act as if they are going to cry.

It's important to remember that not all children will behave badly. For those who do, though, after you've determined the outcome, gently and compassionately reveal to the child once more what's going on, saying something like, "I see that you're having trouble with this problem," or "You look like you're getting kind of irritated," and provide a few options of things the child can do, at least one of which should be appealing to them. This helps a youngster feel comfortable again by giving them a sense of control and companionship. Students who are going through something that is typically frightening or dangerous may eventually say, "I'd like help," if they feel that you are truly treating them and understanding them.

2) Establish calm, smooth transitions: Changes in activities should only serve to jolt pupils into a survival mindset. That sense of "uh oh, what's going to happen next" may be closely related to a situation in which a child's happy, loving father may suddenly become a monster after consuming too much alcohol.

When the time and energy are right, some teachers will signal with music, a meditation bell, or a harmonica blowing. Establishing a routine around transitions is essential to ensuring that kids understand:

- what the transition might actually look like,
- what they're supposed to be doing, and
- what comes next.

3) Give praise in public and criticism in private: Children who have gone through complex stress are likely to receive a strike, as well as a parent or guardian, if they get back trouble. For some, on the other hand, "I made a mistake" may mean "I'm totally unlovable." Teachers must therefore be especially discreet when correcting these pupils.

"Nurture the hell away of the kids," as Rick Hanson said in his demonstration at the GGSC SUMMER MONTHS Institute of Teachers. To help the faculty student feel more confident in himself or herself, identify the times when they perform well and highlight them. For example, you may say, "Wow, I like how you sat on the desk for any complete 5 minutes," or "Thank you for helping your classmate." If you want to change the behavior, try to do so in private as much as you can, using a calm voice.

4) Modify the mindfulness exercises in your classroom: Mindfulness has the potential to be an ideal instrument for mitigating the effects of a personal injury. For kids who have dealt with stress, though, it could also be frightening because the practice talks about unpleasant and frightening emotions as well as bodily sensations.

If you use mindfulness in your classroom, you may want to use some additional modifications that were developed by Mindful Schools and the UCSF HEARTS program:

Tell the children that they can close their eyes at the start of the practice if they so choose. Generally, they should glance at the area in front of them so that no one feels ogled.

Have pupils focus on a ball or other object they are holding in their hands, describing how it feels and appears in their palms, rather than how their bodies feel.

Pay attention to the sounds outside the body, such as nearby traffic or cars leaving the school.

A child's experience with mindfulness practice is far more likely to be successful when it is broken down into these fundamental elements, making them slightly better prepared for application in the future.

5) Look after your own needs. Actually, this should be at the top! This example generally makes the metaphor of getting your mouth and nose mask on first, then putting it on a child, most clear.

Acknowledgements

Behold the magnificent triumph of this extraordinary book, a testament to the divine intervention of God Almighty and the unwavering love and support of my cherished Family, devoted Fans, avid Readers, loyal Customers, and dear Friends. Their ceaseless encouragement has paved the way for this resounding success.

www.ingramcontent.com/pod-product-compliance
Lightning Source LLC
Chambersburg PA
CBHW030557080526
44585CB00012B/410